Remodeling the Zen Master's Kitchen

Remodeling the Zen Master's Kitchen

Poems by

Jeremy Cantor

© 2025 Jeremy Cantor. All rights reserved.
This material may not be reproduced in any form, published,
reprinted, recorded, performed, broadcast,
rewritten, or redistributed without
the explicit permission of Jeremy Cantor.
All such actions are strictly prohibited by law.

Cover design by Shay Culligan
Cover image by Oriento on Unsplash
Author photo by Harvey Gendler

ISBN: 978-1-63980-895-3

Kelsay Books
502 South 1040 East, A-119
American Fork, Utah 84003
Kelsaybooks.com

for
Serafina the Dragon Rider,
Abigail the Star Seeker,
and Marsha, who saved so many

Contents

Foreword

The True Spirit	13
Remodeling the Zen Master's Kitchen	14
The Songbirds	15
Bird-Watching	16
The Caregiver's Song	17
What You Don't Know	18
Posture	19
Women in the Hospital Waiting Room	20
The Arrow of Time	21
There Is Nothing Like a Berkeley Estate Sale	23
Her Husband Considers the Words of Picasso	25
Capitulation	26
Sleep Well	27
Life Force	28
Carrion	29
Remaining Embers	30
Cirrus Uncinus	31
The Campaign	33
Election Day	34
Election Results	35
Sierra Juniper	36
Parallel Key Modulation	37
Found in the Guest Book at the Rented Beach Cottage	39
On the Woodward Avenue Line	40
The Wheels of Progress	41
Two Houses	43
At the Wedding	45
Make-Up Poetry	48
Keepsake	49

Observers	50
Grasses	52
Maturation	53
Reflections on Sibling Rivalry	54
Table for Two	56
Perspective	58
Abscission	59
Coal Seam Fire	60
Marketing Failure	61
The Hummingbird	62
What Do You See?	64
Obeisance	65
Terroir	67
Fickle Muse	68
Windblown	70
New Year's Resolution	72
Prayer	73
End of the Anthropocene	75
Thoughts on Reading My Mentor's Death Poem	76
Taking the Long View	77
Envy	78
Lighthouse Lens	79
A Toast	83

Foreword

"Publishing a volume of verse is like dropping
a petal into the Grand Canyon."
—Don Marquis

And publishing a second is like retrieving it, reclaiming its initial worth and expanding its reach through its own means. In Jeremy Cantor's first collection, *Wisteria from Seed,* we were swept in a strong current of scientific naturalism spotted with reflective pools and warming eddies. As I wrote in the foreword to that set "it finds universals in the quotidian . . . its meaning disguised in the plain dress of moment-to-moment experience." Among the things that stand out in that work is the author's embrace and expression of faithfulness, most clearly stated in that volume's eponymous poem:

I never thought myself a man of faith
yet I grow wisteria from seed

And one senses security, an attitude of comfort to be found even in the fatuous frolicking of dogs with whom "Together we will run and run."

The present volume, Cantor's second, has matured to even greater measurement of the moment—and what momentous *momenti* we recently have—embracing the now with a mixture of rumination and recrimination, more crepuscular in hue than *Wisteria* . . . yet still luminous in its attention to nature, family, community, observation . . . and survival. Wilfred Owen's famous remonstrance that "All the poet can do today is warn" finds voice here, not in such bombastic decrees but in subtler tones of admission, even submission. For this reader, Cantor is most effective when he leads us by the hand into the ordinary to show us its beauty by encouragement, not insistence or rhetorical festooning—what I've referred to as the stealth epiphany. That gentle technique (and its poetically robust impulse) is herein applied generously and to equal effect but is less epiphanic than apotheotic—might one mint "apopoetic" to describe it. These poems are from a farther point in their author's journey, and like their predecessors are skillful compositions of thought and feeling that funnel the reader to their destinations. Where they start is sometimes a place among birds, among patients, among mythic samurai philosopher-swordsmen; in nature red, in nature green, nature didactic, whose lessons are ingested and reissued in art, but nature, unmistakable. Where they arrive is somewhere yet beyond where they end, perhaps some tomorrow:

> *while I continue to perfect my art,*
> *writing of lesser things, like love and death*

This is poetry of time for a time: for our time, mourning traditional truth in the post-truth world; for any time, a sober reconciliation of present with past where memories and reflections admit a darker but no less faithful conviction.

Michael Manning,
former Classical Music Critic/Arts Correspondent
The Boston Globe
June 5, 2025

*May my trembling song
draw death away from my nest
for just long enough*

The True Spirit

> *To write this book I did not use the law of Buddha or the teachings of Confucius, neither old war chronicles nor books on martial tactics. I take up my brush to explain the true spirit...*
> —Miyamoto Musashi, *The Book of Five Rings* (1645)

Like Miyamoto Musashi writing to Kojiro Sasaki,
saying he was very sorry but the duel
they had both been looking forward to
would not take place that day because Musashi
required more time to perfect his art

(which when they met at last was so well-honed
that though he'd brought two swords, he did not use them,
drawing them only afterward in triumph
after crowning Sasaki with a stick)

I regret to inform you
that the topic I've long wished that I were good
enough to write about will have to wait

while I continue to perfect my art,
writing of lesser things, like love and death

Remodeling the Zen Master's Kitchen

I expected to find him
living on brown rice and miso
and to want a kitchen designed accordingly.
I was surprised to learn that
he did not, and did not.
He said "You are surprised only by
what contradicts your expectations.
Do not expect anything,
and you will never be surprised
or disappointed."
I said, "Then should I expect nothing?"
He replied, "No.
What I said was 'Do not expect anything.'
Now get to work."

The Songbirds

They leave familiar footprints—three toes forward,
one toe facing back, the leg constructed
so as to grip the perch without a thought,
involuntarily, whenever the legs are bent—
nor does a songbird have to worry if
the branch he's perching on should disappear
from under him without a moment's warning

He won't claw wildly for the support
that suddenly betrays him—even as
he spreads his wings and straightens out his legs,
his toes release the branch without a thought

I was mistaken when I chose this twig,
this branch, this tree, this forest full of songbirds
this place that I imagined I'd call home
at last—it's not the place I thought it was

I try to grab the trunk and slow my fall
while branches scrape my skin and scratch my eyes
and opaque layered leaves obscure my sight
but still I see the songbird, unconcerned

Everything he'll ever need to know
when everything he counted on is gone
is in his tendons and his hollow bones

His birthright is the art of letting go;
mine is to have faith in what betrays.

Bird-Watching

Nearly-grown fledgling,
still expecting to be fed,
makes the "Feed me!" noises
and fluffs out its feathers
in the quick-vibrating "Feed me!" gesture.

Parent bends over
picks a seed up from the ground
and pops it in the mouth of big baby
who gulps down the seed
without breaking stride
stopping only long enough to swallow.

They haven't gone two steps before
they do it all again.

We're entering the endgame.
The birds feeding their young
won't notice anything, just like
last time.

At least that's what the birds told me
and that includes the birds
who took the opportunity
to peck their neighbors to death
last time.

The Caregiver's Song

though without sufficient breath
to return your ember to flame
I inhale as deeply as I can

aim my lips with care
and blow
though I know

that I consume
that much faster
my own remaining air

What You Don't Know

It feels like the season's last rain
the last rain before the living sweet green

on the hills turns first to the golden brown I love
then to the grey brown I don't understand

the still night air encourages a cloud
of the orange tree's scent

to come out of hiding, envelop the house,
creeping even as far as my open window

around the corner on the south wall
if you stood by me you would not smell it

they could not figure out how else to stop
the little girl's nosebleeds so they cauterized

and left scar tissue covering the nerves
now seventy years later I can count on one hand

the number of things you can smell
and that number does not include

the smell of orange blossoms at night
or the smell of the rain that is about to fall.

Posture

Watching how each patient walks into
the waiting room, I try to guess just where
it hurts, and even try to guess how much.
First comes one who might stand straight again
if he could be convinced it's worth the pain.
Next comes one, more bent, who stood up straight
many years ago for the very last time.
When I get up I will remind myself
again (as all my life I've had to do)
that I have a right to stand up straight,
and (as all my life I've had to do),
again I'll fight the fear that somebody
will holler out a challenge to my right
to stand up straight, to take up that much space.
Another walks in now, almost on tiptoe,
as if trying not to tear the rice paper.

Women in the Hospital Waiting Room

The one with the big legs and arms, whose ringtone sounds like four rising glissandi played on a celeste

The one with the stoop, the slightly bowed legs and the black-framed glasses, who is writing on a touch pad

The one with freckles, age spots like mine and wire-rimmed glasses, who is tapping her foot to a tune only she hears, and next to her, a woman with her sunglasses on top of her head, who might be her daughter, now putting on ChapStick

The one with the red ribbon on her walker and wearing sunglasses indoors, with a man whose speech when addressing her suggests he is not yet accustomed to her deafness

The one with the single long thick chestnut braid

The one in very short shorts who is here with the man who looks like he might be her brother, and the medical assistant asked her "Do you get nauseated or dizzy easily?" before letting her into the examination and surgery area with him

The one with the long exuberantly exploding mane of frizzy hair that I like, just like the hair that my wife and her hairdresser work ceaselessly to make look otherwise

The one I won't glance up at now that my wife has returned to the waiting room, though a friend has told me that a woman can sense even her man's successfully suppressed urge to look

The Arrow of Time

As soon as her mother began to follow
the nurse out of the waiting room
toward the doctor's office
the almost-two-year-old girl
(to be known herein as "Twin One")
began to wail, punctuating her virtuoso solo
with the occasional perfectly-timed
and perfectly-tuned ear-splitting shriek.
While Twin Two calmly played with the blocks,
their father had a brief success
with Twin One when he offered her a sip of water.
A man in his eighties smiled and said,
"Just wait until they're fifteen.
I know. I raised five daughters."
Another old man came back out into the waiting room.
As his wife helped him put his sweater on,
he said "I won the battle, but I lost the war."

The twins' father and grandmother
decided to take them for a stroll.
Twin One resumed her crying.
As soon as Twin Two realized
she was being buckled into her stroller,
she started crying too.
A nearby woman who was looking at her phone
set it down on her lap
and stuck her fingers in her ears.
I closed my eyes and fell briefly asleep
despite the noise,
having raised two boys.

Later, on my way out, I passed
a quiet, ancient woman
with white hair like a river
that has reached the waterfall's brink
and is beginning its descent
through the blinding sunlight.

There Is Nothing Like a Berkeley Estate Sale

her microscope (brass barrels)
her short-wave radio (vacuum tubes)
her slide rule (ivory-faced)
her mechanical polar planimeter (does anyone still make those?)
one copy of every journal her work appeared in

books inscribed to her by most of the famous people in her field
boots, butterflies, black and white photographs
boxes of things I looked at for an hour
but can't recall now

a monkey's skull studded all over with
round silver ornaments like upholstery tacks

sheet music for piano
an oboe reed
an mbira
a djembe

dictionaries in four languages
novels in three
poetry in two

dust the agent missed when cleaning for the sale

two shelves of journals
with entries in two different hands
except for the last volume
with entries in hers only

a wedding ring

her underwear which of course
she needed until the day she died
but there was no one left who
cared enough to get rid of it
before the sale

back at the car you said *Please, love—
don't let that happen to me.*

Her Husband Considers the Words of Picasso

Disciples be damned. It's not interesting.
It's only the masters that matter.
—Pablo Picasso, quoted in Michel George-Michel,
  De Renoir à Picasso (1954)

The candle light's too dim for me to read
your papers scattered on the kitchen table
but even in full daylight I would not
be able to understand the things that you
know more about than anyone else alive.
All of it will die the day you die.
You have no disciples.

But now that you are talking of your work
I won't interrupt you just to tell you
that without you
my life would be a language without metaphor

and I won't interrupt you just to say
that I can't stop myself from thinking about
the fire that still burns behind your eyes,
about your hands, your hair, your lips, your breasts
and about this candle going out.

Capitulation

Today as I got dressed to take a walk,
you bent to your sad twice-daily task,
taking care of wounds that never heal

you briefly looked as if you might, again,
apologize for crying, but instead
just told me I should hurry up and leave.

We've raised our children; I have written poems;
I've even written poems our children like
but my prayers for you remain unanswered.

You're no longer strong enough to help me
hold the boundaries keeping back the world,
which, when it has studied our defenses

and is satisfied it knows at last
our weakness better than we know our strength,
will show us, calmly, patiently, its warrant

entitling it to enter where it will,
to blow in through the door we cannot bar,
bringing wind and rain and weeds and rust—

then we will only answer, "If you must,"
and perhaps, add softly, "Bring the dust."

Sleep Well

The owl circles the boarded-up farmhouse once and leaves
it's been empty for years

nothing remains inside that I would expect
an owl to be interested in

except perhaps rodents who chewed their way in
and live there now, preferring it

to the exposure of the surrounding fields,
plywood over the windows shutting out

visions of tearing fur and cracking bones
which they, as long as they remain inside,

need never know, but still
would rather sleep without dreaming of.

Life Force

The jackrabbit appeared suddenly
in front of my car

its crushed hindquarters carrying
the memory of the previous car

as it dragged what was left of itself
across the road with its forefeet

trailing blood on the pavement
trying to escape the next car, mine,

as if that could make any difference now—
still, its ears stood straight up

Carrion

The boy died when his bicycle spun out
rounding the intersection on the downslope
just missing the turn

into the schoolyard driveway.
Years later people still leave flowers,
photos, a set of handlebars

I saw a vulture circling over the spot today
as if picking up the scent of a memory,
not understanding that it is all over

Remaining Embers

the gates rusted shut
the temple grounds abandoned
I still pray, outside

Cirrus Uncinus

Literally "curly hooks," the pretty wisps,
more than four miles up in bluest skies
where Messrs. Celsius and Fahrenheit shake frigid hands,
the clouds that I call mares' tails
may warn us of rain, or they may not.
A pair of forward-facing eyes may warn
the oriole of predatory danger,
or they may not, but the oriole
won't take the time to think it over,
a neurologically economical
defensive system, saving brain power
for feats of navigation (up from Mexico),
and feats of architecture (weaving nests
suspended from the undersides of palm fronds),
feats that I can't even dream of. This time
the predator-eyed creature's only me,
perennial observer, but the oriole
shows no interest in learning that distinction.
She only knows I'm unpredictable.
She sees my open eyes, waits on the fence,
waits perhaps for me to shut my eyes,
to forget her, fall asleep, to leave,
to die. Her bolder mate lands at the feeder
and I shut my eyes in hope that he
will stay, but when I glance up he is gone
before I can even focus my predator's eyes.
He tries again ten minutes later, but,

seeing my open eyes, he executes
a mid-flight U-turn and is gone.

I go back in and listen to the news
and in the morning's cold sky
is the uncertain, gentle warning of mares' tails.

The Campaign

Let's play dress-up!
he declared with a smile.
Let's put on the robe
and raise the torch
like the lady in New York Harbor!

They could see that he looked nothing like her
but that morning he had promised them
that they finally could realize their lifelong fantasy
of murdering everyone who wasn't just like them
so they shouted out that he indeed was she
and sawed through the feet
of the gift from France
and pushed it over.

He bent over and looked approvingly
where the acid he'd encouraged them
to throw was eating through her copper face
and murmured to her
Relax, it will all be over soon.

Election Day

The meanest boy on the playground
meandered in my general direction,
demonstrating just for me that he
was in no hurry, maintaining an eye-lock
so that I could not possibly mistake his intent,
so he could enjoy my fear to the fullest.
He was the boy who was famous for stealing
everybody's lunch money, and now that same everybody
was patting him on the back as they passed
with an "attaboy!" as he drew his switchblade
from his pocket, his eyes never leaving mine even
as he flicked it open and they all murmured what
a great guy he was and they would always
be right behind him because he had
promised to buy them lunch.

Election Results

(with thanks to Mark Granovetter, author of "Threshold Models of Collective Behavior," *The American Journal of Sociology,* Vol. 83, No. 6. (May, 1978), pp. 1420–1443.)

A wants me dead and says so.
B wants me dead, but will not say so
until he hears *A* say so.
C wants me dead but will never say so,
though he'll gladly vote for that result.
D wants me dead but says he doesn't.
E does not want me dead but
is willing for me to be killed if
that will get him what he wants.
F does not want me dead but
is willing for me to be killed
because *A, B, C, D,* and *E* have
told him that it will get him what he wants.
G doesn't care one way or the other
but is scared of *A, B, C, D, E,* and *F,*
H doesn't want me dead but is
scared of *A, B, C, D, E,* and *F* and is
disappointed by *G*.
And *I* . . .

(The American press calls that
"a polarized electorate.")

Sierra Juniper

Inspired by a photograph (©2021 Christopher Collier) by botanist Christopher Collier. Used by permission.

The wind suggested that I take its shape
and hold it ever after, demonstrating
to all viewers my submission. I've
seen others do that, seen their shape admired
or pitied as the case may be. But I
refused and swore I'd stay upright and dared
the winter wind to do its worst. It killed
all buds that grew out on my windward side
and all I'd left were leeward, branches pointing
in the wind's direction, demonstrating
to all viewers not quite submission,
but perhaps an accusation, indirect,
not pointing toward the frigid enemy
but at the damage I saw done to others.

Parallel Key Modulation

Today she doesn't know she's
humming in a minor mode all day
a song that was written in a major.

If I told her she had dropped
the third degree a half-tone
she'd have no idea what I was talking about.

If she were to hear me doing the same
with a song that she knew well
she would notice that there's *something* wrong
but would not be able to say
just what the trouble is.

(Here the Russian language would distinguish
between a *something* that is not known
and a *something* that is known—
does *something-or-other* do the job
for Anglophones?)

I miss those days when
something-or-other was not right.
What is wrong is all too clear today,
even through the swirling embers,
sparks and smoke.

The fire from which
there's no escape approaches.
Having run out of things to do
we busy ourselves with number games—
each time we see another tree
vanish in a sheet of flame,
we subtract one.

Found in the Guest Book at the Rented Beach Cottage

The only entry
in the young groom's handwriting—
Ah, my sweet gazelle!

On the Woodward Avenue Line

She was sixteen.
She was lovely.
She knew her way
around Detroit.
She sat in the bus,
empty except for herself
and the driver.
A man got on.
Though all the other seats
were vacant,
he sat down next to her.
She picked up
nothing sexual
at all,
nothing predatory
at all.

He talked about the conservatory,
about the art museum.

"So," she said to him,
"are you from Canada?"
"How did you know?" he asked.

She called out to the driver
who had been worrying about her,
It's okay!

The Wheels of Progress

I'm waiting for the farrier
the wainwright and the wheelwright,
all rolled into one—the man
who's working on my car.

He's also the tribologist
(a specialist in friction),
a sometime electrician,
electrochemist and physicist
and guy who turns the wrench.

We trust our fragile bodies
to these piles of glass and steel,
and we trust our piles of glass and steel
to automobile mechanics,
which sometimes is a better bet
than trusting fragile bodies to
our own erratic judgement as
we drive our glass and steel
sometimes to end as piles
of glass and steel and blood

If I'd been waiting for the farrier
two hundred years ago,
would I have been a worrier
imagining how I could be
dumped by a stumble,

scraped off by a branch,
or thrown to the road?

If I am now a worrier it's only
because now I have something to lose.
I'll be home soon, love.

Two Houses

Last year I built myself a treehouse in
a Manitoba Maple. In the fall
I saw its seeds go whirlybirding past
my platform, so I know the tree is female.

A sugar maple would have had both sexes
on one tree, but my tree is "dioecious"
from the Greek words for "two houses,"
the sexes always found on separate trees.

Weak wood and many eager seeds are traits
that don't endear my tree, *Acer negundo*,
to loggers or to lumber mills. It seems
that Europeans couldn't think of any
uses for it, though the Anasazi,
Cheyenne and Ojibway used the wood
and sap to make flutes, bowls and medicine.

I used it to support my home away
from home in our backyard since I could not
evict our Irish Setter from his doghouse
in good conscience—his need's as great as mine.

When my parents' marriage started circling
the drain, my mother said to me one day,
"Married people shouldn't live together—
they should live next door, in separate houses."

I like to think our marriage turned out better
but to be fair I ought to build another
treehouse, one that's just for you to use
when one tree hasn't room enough for two,
when you would like to get away from me
and everything that looks like home to you.
I could get to work on it today.

There's a willow tree across the yard—
I hope that will be far enough away.

At the Wedding

Despite the drought
the hills behind the clubhouse
are green and the Monterey pines are
so tall that even way back here
among the rows of folding chairs
I have to lift my eyes to see the pair of ravens
in their crowns

(why did I let you talk me into
buying a suit I don't want and can't afford
just to wear to this wedding I don't care about?)

that groomsman was so kind to take off his jacket
despite the chill and drape it over
the ninety-year-old woman in the wheelchair
(while the guitarist played a tolerable jazzy arrangement of
the Fauré pavane)

I liked the service which included
nothing absurd or impossible but was sweet
as were the vows, which the couple had written themselves
(I can't remember ours, can you?)

But I don't recall hearing "in sickness and in health"
which is where we've been for years now,
with something so rare nobody but the specialist
has heard of it
and even she has never seen a case like yours

but you will once again tell me
at 2:00 AM that you
have wanted me many times recently but not told me
and I will once again tell you
that if you never tell me then that is as good as not
but I can still remember when every time
seemed not only better than the last time
but the best ever

(after the ceremony a double scotch straight up
helped quite a bit
I didn't ask for a double but the bartender
could see I'm not a guy who can afford
the stuff he poured me with a wink)

and the bride's gown was amazing, even I thought so
and the bride's father of course gave away the bride
but later
after speeches by the groom's brother
and the best man
and the groom's parents
and the maid of honor
and the bride's father,
the bride's mother gave away the bride in her own way
by telling her daughter
"I loved you first but he will love you best"
and I finally cried

(did I tell you that you were gorgeous in that outfit
you thought wasn't classy enough for that crowd?
though we were in a ballroom filled with
rich & pretty women one third our age
you were the only one who took my
breath away especially much later at 2:30 AM
when you told me
you still want me)

Make-Up Poetry

In one of those moods, you asked, "If I were kidnapped,
would you even try to get me back?"

I did my best to answer you. Remember?

"If you were taken from me, Homer's thousand
Achaean ships were but a night patrol compared
with what I would unleash upon your captors:

First, the thousand ships your face would launch,
starting you just even with fair Helen

Next, another thousand for your sweet
and smould'ring voice that wakes me in the morning

Third, another thousand for your wit
that unties Gordian knots before breakfast

Another thousand for your achingly
magnificent and glorious body I
can not describe with any word but "regal"

Finally—for the impossibility
of the coincidence of all those gifts
being combined in just one single woman
who impossibly, against all odds
loves me, I'd leave my armor rusting
on the beach and *swim* the sea to Troy!"

"All right," you sighed, "I guess we're still OK."

Keepsake

you wrote fine essays
but I kept the pillowcase
that you scribbled on

Observers

Hovering would exhaust the scrub jay, yet
all summer it has studied the hummingbirds

as they fed in mid-air, without perching,
to see what might be learned.

Now, instead of clinging upside-down
to the bottom of the suet cage and pecking,

it flies straight at the suet and jabs its beak in,
managing to hover for a half-second's time,

then immediately descends to the ground
to pick up whatever it was able to dislodge.

It is strenuous and inefficient,
but better than going hungry.

A squirrel studies the procedure
to see what might be learned.

My father told me nothing of his youth,
so all I know is what my mother told me,

though he stayed with us throughout my growing years,
trying to figure out what a father

and a husband is supposed to be. I heard nothing
about lessons he might have gleaned

from his successes and mistakes, so I
just watched, to see what might be learned.

The squirrel and I noted each other's presence
then went about our respective businesses,

wondering if, from watching those unsure
of what they did, anything could be learned.

Grasses

"In this climate there's no snow to flatten
last year's spring and summer's grass," I said
as we walked along the meadow's edge.
I told my sons, "We've seasons, yes, but not
the sort you're used to. Winter's just the time
when spring and autumn overlap. In January,
first you'll see hints of green along the ground.
When the young have reached the shoulders of
the standing dead, pointillistic gray
and green will paint the hills to the horizon.
After that the new grows taller than
the old, and green becomes the only color
you can see for miles. Last year's gray grass
and leaves will fall and rot and feed the new."
After that we walked a while in silence
as I thought, "How tall my boys are growing!"

Maturation

We'll have a good backyard crop of lemons this year
though one of the trees has tired of being a dwarf,
ignoring the shortening effect of its carefully chosen rootstock
and reaching past the neighboring trees toward the sun.

The last time I saw such a thing in our yard
it turned out to be not a bolting dwarf but rather
a branch growing out from below the graft,
a trunk from the huge-thorned fruitless rootstock.

Having neither experience nor training
it took me several years to realize what was happening,
and when I did I pruned it off, but this time it's the real thing,
a little thing reaching for the sky, certain of success.

I don't know if even my pole pruner
will reach high enough to bring down
the tall tree's lemons. I may just have to wait
until the tree decides to let them go.

Reflections on Sibling Rivalry

I'd guess the California scrub jay brood-mates
fighting in our yard have never heard of
primogeniture. I doubt they can
recall which one of them was first to hatch.
They won't agree to split the yard between them,
and neither gains the upper wing for long.
After a few hours they'll fight again.

When my sons fought, on those rare occasions
when I'd been able to observe, unseen,
which brother had begun the fight, it always
was the one protesting afterward
with the greater outraged indignation
who had started it. The most dramatic
were the ones conducted, perhaps staged,
just for my benefit. I confirmed that once, by
walking out the front door at the moment
a chair was on the verge of being swung
in a bone-cracking attack. When I
returned, no bones were cracked, no goose-eggs raised,
and the crockery was not in shards.
All was peaceful—nothing out of place.

I don't think the scrub jay siblings care
whether or not I watch them fight but just
in case, I will not stand here at the window
any longer—I'll go take a walk
as I wonder if the scrub jay siblings'
parents ever looked beyond their own
reflections in the windows of our house
and watched our fledglings fighting in our nest,
then looked again, and wondered where they'd gone.

Table for Two

The ground was baked too dry
for an earthworm to venture
close enough to the surface
for the robin to find it,
so she kept out of the grass
and pecked for insects in the wood chips
while her mate stood guard
in the tree overhead
and I smoked my pipe
and watched.

A pair of scrub jays had established their claim
to the territory the year before
by force of wings, beaks, claws and squawks
but now the robin's foraging
did not appear to threaten their claim,
as they did not resist the incursion,
though a jay's occasional flight across the yard
may have been intended to remind the robins
of who it was that really owned the property.

The male robin did not sing
his beautiful song, and did not
fight with his reflection in our window,
having important duties to perform,
but, beyond that, nothing more to prove.

Meanwhile I, with nothing more to prove,
will continue to take care of you as well as I can
in this house with our
broken empty eggshells underfoot.

Perspective

"I have no regrets"
"I would do it all again"
those are not the same

Abscission

> *1. The action or process of abscinding; a cutting off or
> violent separation.* literal *and* figurative
> *2. The state of being cut off; separation and removal.*
> —*The Oxford English Dictionary,* Second Edition (1989)

Is it too sentimental to suppose
that somewhere in the woods where no one goes
amid Fall's red and golden glow there grieves
a tree with no more use for this year's leaves?

Coal Seam Fire

The vaults and passageways were built and dug
not for the purpose that they serve today

not to feed a fiercely living thing
that still, these many decades, won't decay

and die; no, for a purpose not forgotten
but irrelevant. Instead, the honeycomb

beneath the ground allows the coal fire breath
and life. The fire burns, now in the open,

now subterranean and out of sight,
except for crystals (never seen before)

that grow along the edges of the cracks
through which the smoke and heat softly escape,

leaving (for discerning eyes to see)
things brilliant, angular and beautiful.

Marketing Failure

The mockingbird performed his set list several times.
A shirt would be appropriate—a tee
announcing to the world that I had been
to all of this year's concerts, on my back
the bold text header "Mockingbird Tour, 2022"
with the dates and cities listed, as:

July 7 A Tree in My Yard
July 11 A Different Tree in My Yard
July 12 A Neighbor's Tree

and so on.

Long ago I got too old to stand
through rock concerts, so I sat,
admiring the virtuoso. If
I'd gone indoors he would not have noticed.
His performance wasn't meant for me.
I should have a tee shirt made with text proclaiming
"Not the Target Audience"
(eventually applicable to everything).

The Hummingbird

no holds barred
give no quarter
take no prisoners
tolerate no challenge

defend to the last
the food supply
for this year's family
(he's already forgotten last year's)

monitor the perimeter ceaselessly
(well, almost ceaselessly,
he's doing it alone and
he has to sleep some time)

if we interdicted his supply lines
the warrior would manage
just fine on his own
living off the land

when brave warriors die
they fly to Huitzilopochtli
in his form, the hummingbird—
Huitzilopochtli is so bright
none but the bravest warriors
can look directly at him
and even they can stand to gaze
only through a pinhole in their shield

but what would the hummingbird
in our back yard think
if he knew
we think
he's cute?

What Do You See?

Speaking of the few days' absence of
the hummingbird who usually rules our yard,
she joked "Maybe he was at the art museum."
Now I imagine him hovering before the paintings,
perching on the sculptures, flying in
frustration at his own reflection in
the glass-fronted cases while a docent
says "Sometimes we look for something of
ourselves in art. What do *you* see?"
Loudly our hummingbird thrums, then flies away
to find the Bird-of-Paradise Flower
he remembers having seen by the garden's entrance.

Obeisance

Archaeologists in Egypt have discovered a 2,000-year-old temple in Alexandria dedicated to a cat goddess. The temple was filled with statues of Bastet, a once-fearsome lion-headed goddess whose image changed over time to a domesticated cat.
                    —BBC News, 19 January, 2010

Above my head a spider's spinning for
a living. Just past that I see the arbor's
slats of graying wood, and in-between those
I can glimpse the moving autumn clouds.
Before I sat, I turned the cushion over —
one side is for the cat and looks well-used,
a bit more fur left on it every night.
Her wariness suggests to me she's feral.
She always keeps the whole yard's width between us
otherwise ignoring me completely.
I confess I do not know her sex
so I'll say "she" and "her" from childhood habit.
Since we'd rather look at leaves than fence boards
we let the lowest branches of the *Pittosporum*
grow dense, which must have fooled the house sparrow
into thinking it was safe, though just
a yard above the ground. At the apogee
of a perfect feline launch, the cat grabbed it,
returning to the ground with dinner firmly
in her jaws. She walked away, not with
a cheerful perky gait—still all business.
Had it been an oriole or hummingbird
she'd killed, why then I would have been enraged,
but I remember thinking as I watched,
*The house sparrow is an invasive import
that wrecks the bluebirds' nests to build its own,
and they are many—we've sparrows to spare.*

Since I first discovered evidence
of her nighttime bivouacking on
our now-familiar chair, I have been wondering
if she's grateful, as she might be if
we fed her (which we never do).
Today I found the answer to that question:
mouse remains left at our front door.
That's familiar to people who keep cats
(or are kept by cats, if you ask cats)
but unlike other feline gifts that I
have seen, this one was like a sacrifice
made on an altar, not killed first
then carried there—it was killed right there
on the concrete, to one side of the door.
I could tell because the puddle told me
that the mouse had bled out on that spot,
where the head and entrails had been left
in the usual dainty feline fashion.
But, in the center of the welcome mat,
her greatest gift: the mouse's pelt, one foot
still attached. I felt not only thanked
but honored, almost worshipped, as if her
ancestral memory reminded her
that in the distant past *we* worshipped *them*
and after these millennia the time
had come, at last, to return the favor.

Terroir

those are desert plants—
give them plenty of water
and they will go mad

Fickle Muse

I first saw you where a glen
surprised the green-choked path.

I didn't know how long you'd been under.
You must have ridden the cataract down into

the deep green pool that welcomes it,
but whether in a joyous dive or frightened

fall, I'd no idea. Your speed took you down, deep,
so it must have taken you a while

to find which way was up.
No one was as surprised as I was

when you broke the surface, looking as if
you were about to despair of finding air.

I was even more surprised when
you released your breath not with relief

or with a grunt or exclamation, but, impossibly,
with music—not just a single note,

but whole melodic lines. I'll never know
how I sang with you that song I'd never heard before.

I still believe you knew the pool's downstream side
drained into a subterranean cavern,

accelerating, then vanishing from sight,
and that you never intended to go anywhere else.

That's why I didn't warn you.
But I miss you

and I want to learn another song.

Windblown

The parking lot at the post office was strewn
with rain-wet piles of flowering limbs of pear.
The tree-trimmers working for the city,
who always prune the trees before they bloom
had been surprised by an early spring this year.
Always surprised at how early spring comes,
this year I am even more surprised.

I wanted to choose a flowery branch to bring
home to you, but I'd not brought my shears
and I knew that by the time I went home
and came back with them the workers would
have already gathered up the snowy branches
and hauled them away to the city's compost heap,
which some day will feed some other garden.

Meanwhile, the forty vultures in the eucalyptus,
the big one on the corner that eventually
will drop a limb, which may land on somebody
whose luck ran out, had been sitting through
the downpour, huddled, occasionally trading
places with each other, stepping sideways,
spreading their wings only when necessary.

During a break in the rain the sun came out
with only an hour left until sunset.
A bit of rainbow showed the rain's retreat.
The vultures began to leave the rookery
to make use of the last hour of daylight.
It was still windy, but no more than what
the birds could cope with as they left their tree
in single file, then chose their separate routes,
seeking those whose luck ran out today.

Today the wind blows petals to the ground.
Tomorrow may be calm. I'm glad to see,
remaining on the trees, unopened buds.

New Year's Resolution

(the addict's song)

My inner child knows my inner parent
is a sucker and a fool who never learns

so he waits, as patient as a stone
for my inner parent to decide
he's been too strict,
that this might be a good time
to relax the rules for just a little while.

My inner child is doing life in solitary
but knows that opportunity will come
again (because it always has before),
and he'll receive permission to go out
and play in traffic, play with matches,
run with scissors, stick metallic objects
in electric outlets—and in short,
to court all imaginable destruction.

My inner parent will have difficulty
getting my inner child back into his cell
which may require a week, a month, a year
or more, or may not ever be accomplished,
and will regret, again, the moment's lapse
of vigilance, and swear that in the future
that mistake will never be repeated.

My inner child knows my inner parent
is a sucker, and a fool who never learns.

Prayer

Bear with me if you've never used a signal mirror—
I checked out the geometry—it's right.
Your mirror must be shiny on both sides,
and there must be a small hole—near

the edge or in the center, both will work.
Look at your reflection in the mirror
and hold the mirror so it casts a shadow
on your face. The sun's rays through the hole

will make a bright spot in the middle of
the shadow the mirror casts upon your face.
Adjust the mirror's angle 'til the spot
you see reflected on your face lines up

exactly with the mirror's hole. Look through
the hole. Geometry says you now are shining
a reflection of the sun precisely
at whatever you're seeing through the hole.

If that's an aircraft, you just flashed the sun
directly at it. This gets easier
with practice, but don't do it for a lark—
a conscientious pilot will inform

authorities that someone where you're standing
needs help, and if you're not in serious trouble,
that's like turning in a false alarm.
Is my signal-mirror polished well enough?

Did I, perhaps, just aim my mirror wrong?
Is that the sound of my own blood in my ears
or do I hear, at last, the sound of engines?
Do you suppose we'll have to save ourselves?

End of the Anthropocene

The evolution of our skills outpaced
the evolution of our judgement, so

here we are employing those collective
skills by leaping head-first from the cliff's edge

all together (nearly all together—
some did not come freely to the edge

and needed to be pushed or pulled or shackled
to each other or to us or both),

accelerating toward the rocks below
(at rates we have the skills to calculate),

placing bets (with odds we have the skills
to calculate) on who will live the longest

Thoughts on Reading My Mentor's Death Poem

The amnesiac writing his autobiography
resigns himself to writing only his own eulogy
but finally finds himself barely able to write his own epitaph

I know we went to Vancouver
but only because I have the photographs
I know we raised two children
but only because I can see them

When we first moved here, I could hear at night
the ratcheting sound of the ring-necked pheasants
but since the fields all 'round were cleared
for more houses and the ground scraped bare
the nights are quiet except for the owl
and a sound like a very small animal screaming in the woods

Taking the Long View

it was a good thing
my life did not go as planned—
as I'd made no plans

Envy

I envy the fanatic because he has no doubts
the skeptic because he has no certainty

the dolphin because she moves in three dimensions
the mathematician because she moves in two, but dreams in many
the earthworm because it only needs be concerned with one
the geometric point because it has none but feels no lack

the lion because everyone fears him
the butterfly because no one does

the hawk because he dreams of nothing he cannot do
the ant because she is never lonely

I envy the honeybee because she always knows her way home

Lighthouse Lens

Like giant diamonds, each Fresnel lens is unique. Because the prisms—sometimes more than a thousand per lens—are no longer manufactured, the lenses are difficult and sometimes impossible to repair. As a result, the Coast Guard says, they are virtually priceless.
  —Amanda J. Crawford, "LIGHTHOUSE FRESNELS:
   Restoring gems of maritime history,"
   The Baltimore Sun, September 29th, 2001

1.

They tried to get it out intact but broke it
while replacing it with something modern.
You can't get lighthouse lenses like that anymore
for love nor money—they're antiques,
the arcs of crystal prisms bound together
to channel light to an intensity
that challenges and threatens night itself.

2.

Monsieur Fresnel's new lens was first installed
in 1823 atop "the king of lighthouses,"
Le Phare de Cordouan, on mudflats
more than four miles out to sea, in France—
"phare," after the island Pharos, where
the greatest lighthouse in the ancient world,
at Alexandria, once stood.
But Fresnel's lamp was brighter than the Ptolemeys'—
his lens we call "first order" twelve feet high,
his new light with a five-wicked lamp, and wheels,
and clockwork wound each day to turn the lenses.
Ships' pilots now could see a steady light,
with brighter pulses as the lenses turned,
at twice the distance possible before.

The inventor died not ever knowing his
design would be adopted the world over
the name "Fresnel" known up and down the seacoasts
and the lake coasts of a safer world.

3.

More than three thousand miles from the mudflats
of Courdouan, and more than a century later,
on a sandy cliff-top on Cape Cod,
in the year my mother turned thirteen
a fine first-order Fresnel was replaced—
and broken, leaving only pretty pieces.
Twenty-five more years, and my brother and I
climbed up the stairway to the lantern room
to see what had replaced the big Fresnel.
The climb was easy. I did not yet grip
a cane in the hand that didn't hold the railing.

4.

Mr. Francis, once a fisherman,
rented half his bayside house each summer
to families vacationing by the sea.
A sailor had designed the staircase,
the steepest my brother and I had ever seen.
By day, barefoot on paths of warm white sand,
we carried pails among wild blueberry bushes,
though our pails were really just for show (eat ten, keep one).
Huckleberries too—nearly the same,
but for the frosting underneath each leaf.

By night in the sagging feather bed
we could just see flashes from the lighthouse
and if I held my breath I could just hear
the distant radiotelegraph's Morse code,
sounding over and over through the night,
drifting over blueberries and sand,
arriving, faint, at summer's open window.

5.

Now retired, Mr. Francis sat
all afternoon next to his wife
in front of buckets of fresh clams,
opening their wet shells with his knife.
My mother ate our host's clams raw,
until one year some bad ones made her sick.
She made a full recovery and lived
another forty years or so, outlasting
the old house with its steep staircase, outlasting
the sandy fields of blueberries—
all gone, replaced by newer things,
as was that lighthouse lens, a big first-order
Fresnel lens that lasted from the middle
of the nineteenth century well into the next—
almost a hundred years of service.

6.

That—all that—was long before I met you,
long before the day I realized that
without you the ocean would be dark
and deadly, and my little boat would founder.

7.

Today I live beside a different shore,
a different coast, where there is only one
first-order Fresnel left that still sits on
its wheels and track, and has its clockwork.
It is still intact, but not in use,
the whole lighthouse perfectly preserved,
a tall and glorious museum piece.
At this edge of shifting coastal fog,
some days (like today) an hour's drive
will take me from the pressing summer sun
down to the foggy coast where I will leave
my footprints with the ones already there
among the wild beach grasses in the windblown
sand where no wild blueberries grow.

A Toast

Here's to the song you heard when you
were falling in love but have forgotten
the title and the tune and the lyrics
so even if you fell in love to
some other song you'll
think this song is that song

Here's to the way your heart
shunted your brain onto a side track
and left it where you would have to go
and find it and drive it back into town
the next day or the next year or
maybe not ever

Here's to the way the morning sun
through the curtains on the kitchen window
during breakfast the morning after
suddenly made you think not of Vermeer
but of Edward Hopper

Here's to the surface of the water that
has already crossed into night trying to
reflect the evening sky's indigo but instead
showing you a color you have no name for
that promises quiet if only you will
slip beneath the surface past the point
where you'll hear water lapping at your ears
to where eyes closed or eyes open
is all the same

*I asked the goose why—
she just untied my shoelace,
looked with one eye, laughed*

Acknowledgments

Thank you to the following publications, in which versions of these poems previously appeared:

Anthropocene Hymnal: "End of the Anthropocene"
Benicia Love Poetry Competition: "Capitulation"
CAESURA Ascent || Descent: "What You Don't Know"
Crosswinds: "Cirrus Uncinus"
Cultural Weekly: "A Toast," "There Is Nothing Like a Berkeley Estate Sale"
Feline Utopia Anthology: "Obeisance"
Galatea Resurrects: "The Songbirds"
ISLE: Interdisciplinary Studies in Literature and Environment: "Two Houses"
The Lascaux Prize Anthology: "Her Husband Considers the Words of Picasso"
On Writing in a Dark Time: "Election Day," "Election Results" under different titles
The Owl at Sunset: "May my trembling song"
Prelude: "Thoughts on Reading my Mentor's Death Poem"
Reed Magazine: "The True Spirit"
Stories and Poems in the Song of Life: "Fickle Muse"
Wisteria from Seed: "Remaining Ember" (under a different title)
Written Here—The Community of Writers Poetry Review 2018: "Envy"
YouTube with musical accompaniment by Dr. Robert Gross: "Lighthouse Lens"

About the Author

Jeremy Cantor is a graduate of the Community of Writers summer program in California (2018). His debut collection is *Wisteria from Seed,* with a foreword by former Classical Music Critic/Arts Correspondent Michael Manning (Kelsay Books, 2015). Six poems from *Wisteria* were set to music by Dr. Robert Gross and performed at the Boston Conservatory at Berklee by Pamela Dellal, mezzo-soprano; Michael Manning, piano; and Roy Sansom, recorder. Jeremy was a semi-finalist in the competition for the 2019 Dartmouth Poet in Residence program at The Frost Place (Robert Frost's former farmhouse) and a finalist for the 2017 Lascaux Prize. His work has been published in Oxford University Press' *ISLE: Interdisciplinary Studies in Literature and Environment.*

In high school, nothing terrified him as much as did a blank sheet of paper, and at the University of Michigan (1975) he concentrated on math and science. That may be why he did not begin writing until the age of 50. During his career in laboratory chemistry he made and tested engine oil additives, detergents, and pharmaceuticals; drove a forklift; worked in a full-body acid-proof hazmat suit; tried to keep his fingers working in a walk-in freezer at -40°F; and worked behind radiation shielding. He prefers writing.

www.ingramcontent.com/pod-product-compliance
Lightning Source LLC
Chambersburg PA
CBHW070937160426
43193CB00011B/1722